Fun 15-Minute
Poetry-Writing Activities

by Jacqueline Sweeney

SCHOLASTIC
PROFESSIONAL BOOKS

NEW YORK • TORONTO • LONDON • AUCKLAND • SYDNEY
MEXICO CITY • NEW DELHI • HONG KONG

DEDICATION

° ° ° ° ° ° ° ° ° °

For Pat and Bob Balcom—"Pugma and Pugpa"—
and the "Boyz," of course!

ACKNOWLEDGMENTS

° ° ° ° ° ° ° ° ° ° ° ° ° ° ° ° ° ° °

Liza Charlesworth, Editorial Director, who continues to come up with
interesting ideas for new projects and who helps turn fledgling projects into books
with her experienced guidance and sound advice.

To Liza again—for insightfully pairing me with Danielle Blood, who edits my final manuscripts
so well and with such careful awareness of every book's intent.

Marian Reiner, my agent, who is always behind me on every project
I attempt with her keen insight and encouragement.

Carol Patterson of Boght Hills School, who encouraged my first book "from the road"
and who has reappeared after all these years in the same, supporting way.

Lilian Moore, who still sparkles—and inspires us all.

Cover design by Niloufar Safavieh
Cover and interior illustrations by Margeaux Lucas
Interior design by Solutions by Design, Inc.

ISBN: 0-439-11765-8

CONTENTS

INTRODUCTION

Bring the magic of poetry into your classroom with *Fun 15-Minute Poetry-Writing Activities*! First kids read a model poem, then they follow simple steps to write their own terrific poems! These poetry-writing activities are quick and easy, and the topics fit into any curriculum. The poems—written by favorite authors on topics kids love—are just right for this age group and sure to delight.

Kids will love reading the many fun formats of the poems included in this collection: a poem in the shape of an inchworm; an upside-down poem describing a topsy-turvy world; a poem that spreads across the page like moonbeams, and more. Each poem has its own illustrated, reproducible page so that kids can enjoy the full visual effect.

After reading model poems for inspiration, kids are ready to write! These easy, step-by-step writing activities fit into small blocks of time: in the morning, before lunch, at the end of the day, or anytime kids need a creative boost. The steps provide the structure kids need when faced with a blank page: how to choose a topic, brainstorm for ideas, write the first line, wrap up a poem, and so on. This scaffolding guides young writers through the process, tapping into their imaginations and empowering them to write freely.

It is important that children's earliest experiences with poetry are positive so that they feel confident (and happy!) when reading and writing poetry. The goal of this book is to make these early experiences with poetry successful—and open up new levels of enjoyment and creativity in your classroom.

HOW TO USE THIS BOOK

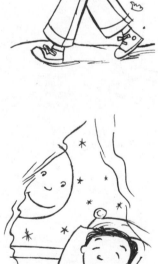

The poems and activities in this book are designed to fit easily into any curriculum. Throughout the year, choose poems and activities to introduce topics of study or simply as a change of pace to spark children's interest. For example, on Earth Day share the poem entitled "Choose a Color," a celebration of the colors found in nature. Or, kick off a unit on transportation with a poem that echoes the roar of the subway.

You can also choose poems that relate to the season, the weather, or even the mood of your students. Brighten up a rainy day with a poem that imitates the rhythm of raindrops. If kids are in a silly mood, why not channel their silliness into a rollicking poetry-writing session using tongue-twisting imaginary words? This collection includes a wide range of styles and topics—there is something for every reader to enjoy.

To prepare for an activity, reproduce the poem page for each student or make an overhead transparency. On each teacher page, you'll find a short section entitled "About This Poem." This provides some background information and tips for sharing the poem. It is helpful to read through this section and the writing steps before doing the activity with your class.

Reading the poem aloud with expression is a great way to gain children's interest. It is a good idea to read the poem a few times (or invite volunteers to read aloud) to give them a chance to absorb the language and meaning. Next, explain to students that they are going to use the poem as a model as they write their own poem. Describe the first of the "Simple Writing Steps" clearly, and then give students a chance to complete the step before moving on to the next one. You may wish to write each step on the chalkboard or on chart paper for easy reference. Give examples whenever you can (there are many examples provided in the book as a starting point).

Encourage kids to write freely, crossing out or drawing arrows as needed. Explain that they will have a chance to copy over or word process their poems when they are finished. Children love to share their work and hear what others have written. From time to time, invite kids to share their writing. This also helps trigger thinking, so that children can build upon each other's ideas.

Students' finished poems make wonderful bulletin board or hallway displays. You can also create a collaborative class poetry book by binding a batch of completed poems with O-rings and adding an illustrated cover. At the end of year, ask children to choose their favorite poem to add to a special collaborative book of "greatest hits."

Fun 15-Minute Poetry-Writing Activities Scholastic Professional Books

Words

I like words like
Lickety-split,
Whacky-doo,
Slippity-slop,
And Hullabaloo.

I like words like
Zippity-zoom,
Zippity-zap,
Gurgly-glug,
And flippity-flap.

I like words that
Twist and jerk
To make my tongue
Do some work.

—Jill Eggleton

Fun 15-Minute Poetry-Writing Activities   Scholastic Professional Books

Words

Children love the sound of words, even words whose meanings they don't know. When I was a girl, I once heard our then Vice President Spiro T. Agnew use the term "pusillanimous pussyfooters" in a speech. I recall how I loved the feeling of those syllables rolling off my tongue, and nearly drove my family bonkers chanting "pusillanimous pussyfooters" for weeks.

Read "Words" to your class. You might want to put the hyphenated words on the board so children can practice saying them. Ask children if there are any big words they love to say (even if they don't know the meanings), and write those words on the board as well.

1 Divide your class into small groups and have them work together to brainstorm a list of wonderful, lip-smacking words. They can make up their own imaginative, tongue-twisting words, or they can look in a dictionary for multisyllable or hyphenated words that are fun to say.

2 Ask children to think of an opening line to introduce their word lists. For example, "My favorite words are…" or "I love words like…" Then have them continue by adding words from their lists:

My favorite words are

_____

_____

3 Continue the pattern in the second stanza:

My favorite words are

_____

_____

4 Remind children that their poems do not have to rhyme, although it could be fun for them to make up rhyming words as the poet did in "Words." Tell them to focus on words with interesting sounds. If they are stuck, encourage them to keep looking in the dictionary for additional wonderful words.

5 Before they write the final stanza, have children look back at the ending of "Words" for inspiration. Invite children to end their own poems with pizzazz. Suggest that they close their poems by stating the reason they like the words on their list.

Our Washing Machine

Our washing machine went whisity whirr
Whisity whisity whisity whirr
One day at noon it went whisity click
Whisity whisity whisity click
Click grr click grr click grr click
    Call the repairman
    Fix it...Quick!

—Patricia Hubbell

Fun 15-Minute Poetry-Writing Activities   Scholastic Professional Books

Our Washing Machine

ABOUT THIS POEM

"Our Washing Machine" is a delightful poem that rhythmically explores one of life's frustrating moments with machines. Read the poem aloud the first time—just for fun. The second time you read it, ask children to listen for changes in the sounds as the washing machine breaks down. The use of words that imitate the sounds they describe is called onomatopoeia; for example, *plippity-plop* of raindrops or *clackety-clack* of trains. Patricia Hubbell repeats each sound to create a predictable rhythm that also reflects the mood of the poem and the machine!

SIMPLE WRITING STEPS

1 Ask each student to choose a mechanical object or device that he or she has experienced breaking down. Children might choose their blue bicycle, Grandpa's truck, Mom's car, Aunt Ellie's toaster, the classroom pencil sharpener, and so on.

2 Explain that kids will write a poem using made-up sounds to describe their machine breaking down. Have them invent a sound for the object when it's running smoothly. They can use this sound in the first few lines.

3 Next, invite kids to create a sound for their machine breaking down. They can use this sound in the next few lines.

4 Then have kids make up a sound that shows that the machine is dying, such as *cough-wheeze, sputter-spit,* or *crrrackle-hiss.* They can repeat the sound to create the next line or two.

5 For the last line, children can decide what they will do about their broken machine. Can the machine be saved? Who will fix it?

Rain Drops...

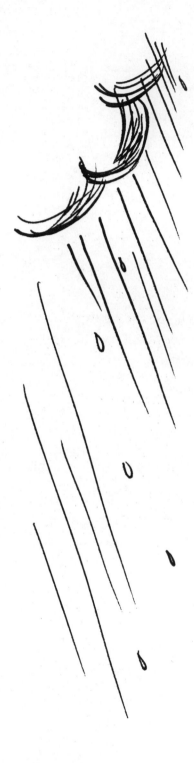

rain
drops
spot
they
spit
on
rock
they
rip
on
trees
rain
drops
tip
rose
buds
all
buds
we
and
good
they
drop
on
hats
and

rap
on
cars
from
clouds
they
flute
down
with
a
long
sigh
and
a
small
song
they
kiss
your
hair
again
again
again
again.

—Sallie Burrow Wood

Fun 15-Minute Poetry-Writing Activities Scholastic Professional Books

Rain Drops...

ABOUT THIS POEM

Weather is full of action—and therefore it's the perfect topic for exploring action verbs. Whether or not you've introduced verbs to children, "Rain Drops..." is a fun way to begin. Ask your class to listen for the action of the rain as you slowly read the poem aloud. On the board, list all of the poem's verbs: *spot, spit, rip, drip,* and so on. Then read the poem again, asking children to "zap" each verb by raising a hand each time they hear one. Read the poem faster and faster (tell them the storm's getting worse), and watch their bodies begin to reflect the action in the verbs.

SIMPLE WRITING STEPS

1 Choose different kinds of weather you'd like children to explore. As a group, generate a list of action verbs to describe each. Write them in columns on chart paper.

snow	*wind*	*sunlight*
floats	*howls*	*sizzles*
flutters	*hisses*	*warms*
freezes	*rattles*	*bakes*
twirls	*shrieks*	*melts*

(This weather-verb pool can be used for many different kinds of writing, so it's useful to hang it on the wall for future reference.)

2 Invite children to choose their favorite weather or aspect of weather (snowstorms, lightning, tornado, thunder, fog, and so on), or ask them to choose a type of weather from a hat. Have them brainstorm their own list of action words for their type of weather.

3 Point out how the form of "Rain Drops..." imitates the path of falling rain. Suggest that kids think about how to make their own poems look like their type of weather. For example, a lightning poem could form a zigzag shape and a wind poem could be written in ripples across the page. Remind children to include as many of the action words from their list as they can.

4 Encourage kids to come up with an ending for their poem that matches their weather type. Have them look at the ending of "Rain Drops...," and point out that the repetitive "again again again again" imitates the repetitive quality of rain falling. Can children play with words in a way that imitates thunder, fog, lightning, and so on?

Sweets

Here
Is a list
Of likely
Words
To taste:

Peppermint,
Cinnamon,
Strawberry,
Licorice,
Lime:

Strange
How they manage
To flavor
The paper
Page.

—Valerie Worth

Fun 15-Minute Poetry-Writing Activities Scholastic Professional Books

Sweets

ABOUT THIS POEM

Valerie Worth's poem opens a wonderfully simple door to exploring the senses through poetry. The key to this poem is to read slowly and savor every word. Be sure to linger on each taste word. After you've read the poem aloud a few times, ask students to share some of their favorite words for tastes or flavors. (Remind them that the words might not always be related to food—for example, toothpaste, pine needles, and so on. Their favorite tastes also might not be sweet. Think sour, tangy, spicy, salty, and so on.)

SIMPLE WRITING STEPS

1 Ask children to choose one of the senses: touch, smell, taste, sight, or hearing. Explain that they will create their own list poem about this sense.

2 Next, have children choose a category for their sense. For example, they might choose soft as a category for touch words. Categories for smell might be spicy, stinky, luscious, and so on.

3 Invite students to think of a list of ten things from their personal experiences that fit the category they chose. For example, soft things might include kitten fur, snowflakes, and flannel pajamas.

4 Show children an example of how to introduce their word lists, such as:

> These
> Are words
> That all
> Mean soft:
>
> _____
>
> _____

Have kids write their own introduction and then include words from their sense list.

5 For the final stanza, invite children to write something about the category that ties all of the sense words together. Have them look back at "Sweets" as an example. Encourage them to cut words, change or rearrange words, and alter the structure in order to create an ending that works meaningfully for them.

Choose a Color

If I were brown I'd be cattail
or turtle deep burrowed
in mud.

If I were orange
I'd be a newt's belly,

If yellow a willow
in Fall.

If pink I'd be a flamingo
or salmon
leaping upstream.

If I were blue
I'd be glacier,

If purple a larkspur
in Spring.

If I were silver
I'm sure I'd be river
    moonshattered
in liquid surprise.

If I were green
I'd be rainforest,

tree canopied.

If green I would help
the world

breathe.

—Jacqueline Sweeney

Fun 15-Minute Poetry-Writing Activities Scholastic Professional Books

Choose a Color

ABOUT THIS POEM

"Choose a Color" speaks for itself as an exploration of colors in nature. You might introduce this poem to celebrate Earth Day. You might also use the poem and prompts when your curriculum demands a quick focus on a particular aspect of nature: endangered species, animals and their habitats, appreciating and protecting the environment, and so on. Have the class read this poem aloud, with each child reading a different verse. Option: Break your class into groups, and ask each group to draw two colors from a hat. These colors are their "If I were" colors. Ask children to think of something in nature that corresponds to those colors. After following the writing steps below, put each group's efforts together to form a collective color poem. And if it's Earth Day, make the poem big, illustrate it, and hang it in the hall!

SIMPLE WRITING STEPS

1 Invite children to choose a color and visualize it in their minds. Then ask them to picture something from nature that looks as if it were painted this color.

2 Next, ask your class to write the following first line and fill in the blanks:

If I were _____, I'd be _____.
               (a color)   (a thing)

If children think of two color comparisons, show them this structure:

If I were _____, I'd be _____.
Or _____.

3 Each of these color comparisons can stand on its own as a stanza. Let children expand their color comparisons with details if they wish. Encourage them to write about as many different colors as they can in the allotted time.

4 Have kids decide the order of the stanzas, saving their favorite one for last. They can make any additional revisions and then write their final drafts.

Comida/Food

Uno se come
la luna en la tortilla
Comes frijol
y comes tierra
Comes chile
y comes sol y fuego
Bebes agua
y bebes cielo

One eats
the moon in a tortilla
Eat frijoles
and you eat the earth
Eat chile
and you eat sun and fire
Drink water
and you drink sky

—Victor M. Valle

Fun 15-Minute Poetry-Writing Activities Scholastic Professional Books

Comida/Food

ABOUT THIS POEM

If you have Spanish-speaking students in your class, ask a volunteer to read the poem aloud for a treat! If not, you read it, for this is a poem for everyone. What child hasn't imagined the moon as cheese or the sun as a lemon lollipop? Children can translate the colors and textures of anything into food, which is what gives this particular poem such appeal. If you have bilingual students in your class, you might ask them to translate their poems or a classmate's poem into their native language; then they can present both versions to the class. Whatever you decide to do, have fun!

SIMPLE WRITING STEPS

1 Ask children to imagine that they are going to eat things they might see in nature: ocean, trees, rocks, stars, clouds, rainbows, fog, and so on. As a class, make a list of 5–10 of these "potentially edible" things. The key is to choose something much bigger than ordinary food!

2 Have kids choose three of their favorite things from the nature list. Then have them decide what foods these things could be. The decision might be based on color, shape, temperature, and so on. For example, stars could be sprinkles and fog could be marshmallow fluff. Remind kids that they can also choose things to drink. Unhinging the imagination and having fun are important in this step!

3 Children might begin their poems this way:

I eat _____ in a
(thing from nature)

_____.
(kind of food)

For example:

I eat stars in a
bowl of popcorn.

I eat snow in
vanilla ice cream.

Or they can use other starting lines, such as:

When I eat _____,
(kind of food)

I eat _____.
(thing from nature)

For example:

When I eat pancakes,
I eat comets.

When I drink an ocean,
I drink…

4 When kids have finished writing all of their "nature snacks," they can revise the order of the stanzas. Remind them to save their best one for last!

Fun 15-Minute Poetry-Writing Activities Scholastic Professional Books

The Blues

When the shoe strings break
On *both* your shoes
And you're in a hurry—
That's the blues.

When you go to buy a candy bar
And you've lost the dime you had—
Slipped through a hole in your pocket somewhere—
That's the blues, too, *and bad!*

—Langston Hughes

The Blues

ABOUT THIS POEM

We don't always think of children as having the blues, but they do—and it's important to encourage children to explore their "blue" feelings. After reading Langston Hughes's poem, ask students what they think "having the blues" means. Then ask them why they think this particular color was chosen. Why not "the yellows" or "the greens"? Explain to children that the blues is one of America's oldest musical forms, and that it has its roots in early African American culture. African Americans began singing the blues because singing about the harsh, daily truths of their lives helped them survive. Hint: If possible, preview and play music of blues artists for children prior to reading the poem. They might enjoy listening to the songs of B.B. King or Albert King.

SIMPLE WRITING STEPS

1 Invite children to make a list of all the things in their lives that give them the blues (losing things, cleaning their rooms, siblings annoying them, being grounded, and so on).

2 Read "The Blues" aloud, and ask your class to listen for the rhythm and music in the flow of the words.

3 Next, ask kids to write as many stanzas as they'd like about their own blues. Have them think of a repeating line to give their poem rhythm, like the line "That's the blues" in Langston Hughes's poem. Demonstrate how to include this repeating line in the same place in each stanza. (The beginning or end of the stanza is a good place.) Remind kids that their poems do not need to rhyme. Provide some

examples to get them started, such as:

When your brother teases
and says it's you
and you get punished—
That gives me the blues.   (This is the repeating line.)

When you save up for pizza
and it comes out cold
and the cheese is rotten
That gives me the blues.

4 Invite kids to share bits and pieces of their poems as they write so that their ideas will inspire one another. Encourage students to write as many stanzas as they wish. When they are writing their final version, children can choose to include their favorite stanzas and arrange them in any order they wish.

Street Song

O, I have been walking
with a bag of potato chips,
me and potato chips
munching along,

Walking along
eating potato chips,
big old potato chips,
crunching along,

walking along
munching potato chips,
me and potato chips
lunching along.

—Myra Cohn Livingston

Fun 15-Minute Poetry-Writing Activities Scholastic Professional Books

Street Song

Fun 15-Minute Poetry-Writing Activities   Scholastic Professional Books

ABOUT THIS POEM

"Street Song" is actually a modern lyric poem. Lyric poems date back to ancient Greece where they were either sung or recited to the accompaniment of a lyre. Explain to children that a lyric poem should be short (one page or less), should express the personal feelings of one speaker (usually the poet), and should give the feeling that it could be sung.

SIMPLE WRITING STEPS

1 As a group, brainstorm a list of eating verbs, using the *-ing* ending—for example, *gnawing, munching, gobbling, slurping,* and so on. Write these on the board as a word bank and label them "Eating Verbs." This is a good opportunity to have kids use a thesaurus.

2 Explain to children that they will write a poem that combines two topics: taking a walk and eating a fun food. Ask children to choose a fun food—preferably one that's small enough to tote. (Although a tall tale approach could prove interesting, too!)

3 Ask students to feel the rhythm of the words and the joy of eating this wonderful food. They might begin by writing a series of *-ing* verbs, such as "munching and crunching and zipping and zinging," or they might go in a different direction.

4 Invite children to begin the first stanza by introducing both topics (walking and eating). For example:

> Here I am _____ ing along, (walking, strolling)
>
> _____ing (crunching, munching, slurping)
>
> my _____. (carrots, nachos, smoothie)

5 They might even write about what they see on their walk. Encourage children to write as many stanzas as they like that will fit on one page. If children get stuck, have them read "Street Song" again for ideas.

Yellow Weed

How did you get here,
weed?
Who brought your seed?

Did it lift
on the wind and
sail
and drift
from a far and yellow
field?

Was your seed a
burr,
a sticky burr that
clung to a
fox's
furry tail?

Did it fly with a
bird
who liked to feed
on the tasty
seed
of the yellow
weed?

How did you come?

—Lilian Moore

Fun 15-Minute Poetry-Writing Activities Scholastic Professional Books

Yellow Weed

Nothing echoes quite so beautifully as a poem by Lilian Moore. She creates this sense of echo by posing questions within the structure of the poem. This poem is also an ode, from the Greek word *aeiden* (to sing). Odes were originally sung and danced to by a chorus. An ode often addresses a person or thing that is not present and sings its praises. Before you read the poem aloud to the class, ask children to imagine the journey of the seed. You might also ask them to listen for clues that reveal the poet's attitude. Does she like this weed? What method does she use to sing its praises? Encourage students to experiment with using questions in their own poems.

1 Tell children that it's their turn to ask questions. Ask them to choose a subject to address—something that sparks their interest: An asteroid? A great white shark? A rain forest creature? A penguin? A tyrannosaurus rex?

2 Put a few question openers on the board to assist children: *Did it...? Do you wish...? Were you...? Was it...? Was your...?* Have children use these openers to write three or more questions they would like to ask their subjects. Tell them to use their imagination and ask questions they are truly curious about. For example:

> Why did you disappear, dinosaur?
> Who took you away?
>
> or
>
> How did you get so green, leaf?
> Who painted your color?

Tell children to pretend their subject is sitting right in front of them and to ask as many questions as they would like. Encourage them to use a conversational tone.

3 Have students arrange their questions in any order they wish, with each question forming its own stanza. They can also play with the arrangement of the words on the page. Have them look back at "Yellow Weed" for inspiration. Does a horizontal or diagonal arrangement work better with their poem than a vertical one? It's up to the poet!

4 If kids get stuck at the end of their poems, suggest that they use one final question, preferably the most compelling one.

Letter to Bee

Bee! I'm expecting you!
Was saying Yesterday
To Somebody you know
That you were due—

The Frogs got Home last Week—
Are settled, and at work—
Birds, mostly back—
The Clover warm and thick—

You'll get my Letter by
The seventeenth; Reply
Or better, be with me—
Yours, Fly.

—Emily Dickinson

Fun 15-Minute Poetry–Writing Activities Scholastic Professional Books

Letter to Bee

ABOUT THIS POEM

Who doesn't love getting letters from friends? Emily Dickinson gives letter writing a jaunty twist in "Letter to Bee." In fact, many of her poems assume this personal, epistolary tone. (*Epistle* is the Latin word for *letter*, and also the name of this type of poem.) You might point out to students that Emily lived a solitary life (in a world without telephones!), which made letter writing especially meaningful to her. Letters were often her only connection to the outside world. This poem offers a delightful way for children to practice their own letter-writing skills while exploring a new poetic form.

SIMPLE WRITING STEPS

1 Have children work in pairs for this activity. Ask each child to choose an animal (or insect) that he or she would like to be. Explain to children that they will write letters to their partner, pretending to be the animals they have chosen. (If you are studying particular animals, you may wish to have children select from these or draw from a hat.) Option: Children can make individual mailboxes (using shoe boxes) with their animal's name and address on them, such as:

> Cynthia Bee
> 40 Hive Street
> Honeyville, Maine

2 Have children begin their poems as if writing a letter: "Dear _____." (Encourage children to come up with fun names such as Frieda Frog, Alvin Ant, and so on.)

3 Children can continue the letter as if writing to an old friend. Perhaps they can include a question or two about the weather, the condition of a habitat, or a common predator.

4 Tell children they might include a feeling or thought by starting a line with *I wish*. Encourage them to use their own wording and have a gabby, fun time!

5 Have kids end the poem the way they would end a letter. You may wish to review common ways to close a letter, such as *sincerely*, *warmly*, *yours truly*, and so on.

6 Finally, kids can place their letters in addressed envelopes and deliver them to their "animal" pen pals!

The Inchworm

I inch, I arch, I march along. I'm just a pinch, a mere inch long. I stroll and stick on sticks in thickets, and never pick up speeding tickets.

—Douglas Florian

Fun 15-Minute Poetry-Writing Activities   Scholastic Professional Books

The Inchworm

"The Inchworm" is a calligram, a special kind of shape poem created by the early twentieth century French poet, Guillaume Apollinaire. A calligram takes on the shape of the thing it's written about. For example, a love poem could be written in the shape of a heart, and a daisy poem could be written in the shape of—you guessed it—a daisy! Calligrams can get a bit tricky when children start writing about whirling tornadoes and erupting volcanoes, but encourage them to have fun experimenting with different forms!

I suggest that you begin by reading the poem aloud to your class. Then show students the poem (you may wish to make photocopies or use an overhead projector). Children love shape poems and will most likely react with delight. Writing their own shape poems offers children a new and interesting approach to poetry and is especially appealing to visual learners. Hint: Have kids write their poems first (sloppy copies!) and shape them later. This allows students to concentrate on one aspect of the poem at a time.

SIMPLE WRITING STEPS

1 First, children need to choose a subject for their poems. Ask students to write about a favorite thing—something that delights, amuses, or intrigues them.

2 Ask children to picture the object in their minds and write the following things about their object:
◎ one or more of its colors
◎ at least two adjectives that describe it (such as *smooth*, *shiny*, or *sharp*)
◎ at least two action words that describe how their object moves (*spinning*, *wiggling*, *sliding*, and so on)

3 Next, have students compose a poem using "like whats" after each color, adjective, or action word. For example:

I am spinning like _____
(an object)

I am fuzzy like a _____
(descriptive word)

4 Ask children to compose a funny or interesting ending. They might begin their last line with *I wish…* or *Someday….*

5 Finally, invite children to rewrite their poems in the shape or motion of their object. For example, they can write a poem about the ocean in the shape of a wave, a poem about a soccer ball in a round shape, and so on. Hint: If a subject suggests a difficult shape, have children use only part of the object. For example, a shark poem might assume the triangular shape of a fin or tooth. Invite students to enhance their poems by using colored pen or pencil and adding a big, bold title.

Topsy-Turvy Land

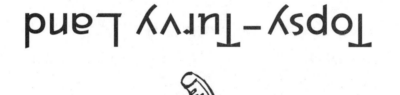

The people walk upon their heads,
The sea is made of sand,
The children go to school by night.
    In Topsy-Turvy Land.

The front-door step is at the back,
You're walking when you stand,
You wear your hat upon your feet,
    In Topsy-Turvy Land.

You pay for what you never get,
I think it must be grand,
For when you go you're coming back,
    In Topsy-Turvy Land.

—H. E. Wilkinson

Topsy-Turvy Land

ABOUT THIS POEM

What is more fun than imagining a world that functions upside down and backward? Not only does this sort of silliness appeal to children, but it also offers them a fun way to create their own imaginary worlds! It's empowering, for example, for kids to portray a world in which adults wear hats on their feet and walk on their hands. Teachers should try this, too! Imagine how good you'll feel writing a poem called "Topsy-Turvy Second Graders!" or "Third-Grade Upside-Downers."

SIMPLE WRITING STEPS

1 First, have children choose a subject—for example, upside-down school (or land, house, planet, zoo, camp, mall, and so on).

2 Ask children to brainstorm a list of characters and things that might occupy the scene of their choice. For example, "Upside-Down School" might include chalkboards, desks, children, teachers, books, buses, and a flagpole.

3 Invite students to imagine how the things on their list would seem if they were backward or even just different from the ordinary. Encourage them to use the five senses as they do this. For example, tulips could taste like strawberries, tree trunks could smell like chocolate bars, dogs could ring, and doorbells could bark.

4 Let children start their poems in their own way. Here are some suggestions if they are stuck:

> In Upside-Down Town
> Flowers grow from the sky.
>
> or
>
> The kids who go to Backward School
> write with their toes.

5 After children have added as many crazy details as possible, invite them to copy their finished poems upside down!

Sky

Tall and blue
true and open

So open my arms have room
for all the world
for sun and moon
        for birds and stars

Yet how I wish I had the chance
to come drifting down to earth—
        a simple bed sheet
covering some little girl or boy
just for a night
        but I am Sky
        that's why

        —Grace Nichols

Fun 15-Minute Poetry-Writing Activities   Scholastic Professional Books

Sky

ABOUT THIS POEM

This poem offers a chance to explore personification (attributing human qualities to something nonhuman). Ask students to try to guess what the poem is about while you are reading it aloud. (Don't tell them the title and don't read the last two lines until they have had a chance to guess the subject.) Point out that the author is pretending that she is the sky and imagining that she possesses the sky's best qualities. See if children can find the describing words the poet chose for her sky (*tall, blue, true, open*). Invite children to close their eyes and picture themselves as the sky as you read the poem to them again.

SIMPLE WRITING STEPS

1 Ask students to choose something large from nature: the sun, the moon, the ocean, a blue whale, a sunset, a bolt of lightning, a redwood tree, and so on.

2 Next, ask children to close their eyes and imagine that they are the thing they chose. Then have them think of four words that best describe themselves as this thing.

3 Ask children to begin their poems with the four describing words. For example, they might begin a poem about the moon with this opening:

> Silver and round
> smiling and bright

4 Invite students to think of what they do best as that thing from nature. For example, the moon might smile down at people or send silver light shining through a child's window. Once children have decided on their special ability, ask them to write about it. Remind them not to say what they are until the very end of the poem.

5 The ending might be a simple statement revealing their identity:

> I am _____.

Option: Play a guessing game! Have children take turns reading their poems aloud without reading the endings. Then other students can guess the subjects of the poems.

whispers

rain
tells me its name
it whispers
round my house

in hushed tones
behind trees
through leaves
it whispers

I am near
I am near

before it is here
rain whispers
round the corners
of my house

—Monica Kulling

Fun 15-Minute Poetry-Writing Activities Scholastic Professional Books

whispers

Fun 15-Minute Poetry-Writing Activities   Scholastic Professional Books

ABOUT THIS POEM

After reading "whispers" aloud, ask children how personification is used in this poem. You might also point out that the poet chose to eliminate punctuation and most of the capital letters. Ask children why they think she chose to do this. Perhaps she wanted to make the poem seem small and quiet, like a whisper. Students will enjoy choosing their own favorite thing from nature and then giving it voice, as Monica Kulling did with rain. This poem is also a fun springboard for using prepositions.

SIMPLE WRITING STEPS

1 Invite students to choose a favorite creature or thing from nature (such as wind, lightning, sunlight, rainbows, waterfalls, leaves, crickets, and so on). While children are choosing, write the following prepositions on the board: *behind, through, around, under, over, onto, into, beside, below, above, beyond, next to, near.*

2 Have children think of three actions that their nature choice does. For example, thunder *rumbles, grumbles,* and *roars*; sunlight *shimmers, sparkles,* and *shines.*

3 Ask children to look at the list of prepositions. These prepositions will help them as they think about where their nature choice exists. Show them how to use their verbs along with the prepositions to form brief phrases. For example, *thunder roars over the hills* and *sunlight sparkles through the windowpane.* Have children write a stanza about each of the actions on their list.

4 Now ask children to decide what their nature choice says and how it says it. For example, thunder growls *I am angry—run away!* Sunlight sings *Don't worry, don't worry.* Have children include this phrase somewhere in their poem. It can be a refrain, or it can be used for their ending. However kids choose to end their poems, remind them to keep the ending simple.

I Want You to Meet...

...Meet Ladybug,
her little sister Sadiebug,
her mother, Mrs. Gradybug,
her aunt, that nice oldmaidybug,
and Baby—she's a fraidybug.

—David McCord

Fun 15-Minute Poetry-Writing Activities Scholastic Professional Books

I Want You to Meet...

Fun 15-Minute Poetry-Writing Activities   Scholastic Professional Books

ABOUT THIS POEM

Remember all those formal introductions you had to endure as a child? "I want you to meet your Great Aunt Sarah" or "You're going to meet your father's boss tonight, so behave yourself." Just once, wouldn't it have been great to hear an introduction that was positively silly? This poem provides a wonderful twist on introductions through creative and humorous rhymes. Encourage kids to use fun, multisyllable animal names in their own tongue-twisting rhymes.

SIMPLE WRITING STEPS

1 Read "I Want You to Meet..." aloud to your class.

2 Write the following list on the board for children to choose from:

hummingbird	manatee
katydid	chickadee
antelope	kitty cat
buffalo	salamander
woodpecker	centipede
honeybee	T. rex

3 After children have chosen a subject, show them the following silly poem to spur their thinking:

My name is Charlie Pelican,
my father's Daddy Fellican,
my sister's little Sallycan,
my uncle's a great big bellycan,
and my dog Rover is a smellycan!

4 Invite children to write their own silly poems. To get kids started, have them brainstorm as many funny, made-up words as they can that rhyme with their animal. Encourage them to make up their own structure and to use their funniest rhyme for their ending.

Hint: It is often helpful to have children work in pairs as they write these poems.

Rules

Do not jump on ancient uncles.

*

Do not yell at average mice.

*

Do not wear a broom to breakfast.

*

Do not ask a snake's advice.

*

Do not bathe in chocolate pudding.

*

Do not talk to bearded bears.

*

Do not smoke cigars on sofas.

*

Do not dance on velvet chairs.

*

Do not ask a whale to visit
Russell's mother's cousin's yacht.

*

And whatever else you do do
It is better you
Do not.

—Karla Kuskin

Fun 15-Minute Poetry-Writing Activities Scholastic Professional Books

Rules

Living in a world brimming with rules isn't easy, especially for children. This poem offers students the opportunity to accomplish a hilarious turnaround: creating a poem that is filled with zany rules of their own invention. Children will enjoy working with a partner to create their "rules" poems, because two minds brainstorming zingers are definitely better than one! "Rules" poems are wonderful read-alouds because they have a natural rhythm built into the structure.

SIMPLE WRITING STEPS

1 After reading Karla Kuskin's poem aloud to students, have them begin brainstorming their own set of rules. Ask them to think of their own sentence-starter to begin each rule, such as *Never, Not allowed to…, Must not…,* and so on.

2 To assist their thinking, write the following phrases on the board:

Never, Must not, You're not allowed to…
pounce on _____
shout at _____
wear _____
swim in _____
take a _____
sit on _____
ask a _____

3 Ask for suggestions to fill in a few of the blanks. This should be enough to get kids going on their own. Encourage children to make up their own phrases and ideas, borrowing only what works for them from the suggestions on the chalkboard.

4 Children can end their poems with their favorite rule or they can make up a general rule, as Karla Kuskin did. If children are stuck, offer some suggestions for a final line, such as *And finally…, Above all else…, Most important….*

Mixed-Up Me

My arms are made of tulips,
My head is made of rocks,
My feet are made of bumble-bees,
So I've no need of socks.

My legs are made of waterfalls,
My chest is made of cheese,
My hips are made of hippopotamuses,
So excuse me while I sneeze.
        AH CHOO!

My middle's made of marble stone,
My neck is made of cookies,
There's sunshine everywhere in me,
In all the crans and nookies.

My eyes are made of forest fires,
My ears are made of thunder,
My nose is made of apple sauce,
My tongue is made of Qund'ar.
        ('Qund'ar' is a magical mountain in Persia.)

My thoughts are made of cross-eyed bats,
My dreams are made of sleeping cats,
I'm all mixed up as you can see,
And all that's here I'm glad to be.

                —Wyoming

Fun 15-Minute Poetry-Writing Activities Scholastic Professional Books

Mixed-Up Me

ABOUT THIS POEM

This poem is just plain fun! It's a refreshing change from the sometimes belabored imagery we feel forced to use in our writing—the kind that requires "oohs" and "ahs" from the audience. This poem just is. Every time I read it, I feel joyful and laugh as I picture a person looking like the character described. You might ask students how they feel about the wonderful assertion at the end: "And all that's here I'm glad to be." Wouldn't the world be a better place if we all felt this way about ourselves—on clumsy days, forgetful days, late days, step-in-puddle days, and bad hair days?

SIMPLE WRITING STEPS

1 As you can see, there is no rhyme or reason to which body part is presented first in this self-portrait. It starts with arms, head, and feet in the first stanza and moves to legs, chest, and hips in the next. I suggest that you allow children the same freedom to explore. Tell them to write about themselves and begin anywhere they wish.

2 On the chalkboard, write a list of body parts that you consider appropriate. Don't forget to include the heart, mind, brain, stomach, bones, veins, and so on. It's also fun to include thoughts, dreams, wishes, and hopes.

3 To get children started, suggest that they use a relaxed format similar to "Mixed-Up Me":

   My _____ are made of _____ ,
   My _____ is made of _____ ,
   My _____ are made of_____ ,

4 Should children rhyme lines 2 and 4, as in the model? It's completely up to them. Their poems will work either way. The goal is to create wildly funny and interesting comparisons, whether or not they rhyme.

5 Encourage children to close their poems with a short, creative, or funny ending. Finally, have them personalize their poems with a title such as "Silly Sarah," "All About Andrew," and so on.

I Want to Swim

I want to swim.
Really swim.
Not just splash my arms
and legs and sink
but swim.

I want to dive.
Really dive.
Not just smack the water
with my feet,
but dive

headfirst
from poolside,

bubbles swirling
'round my body
as I glide.

And topside
when I shake the hair
from my face,
pinch the water
from my eyes,

I'll finally see the others
far behind.

Let my feet be flippers,
arms be fins.

I want to swim.

—Jacqueline Sweeney

Fun 15-Minute Poetry-Writing Activities Scholastic Professional Books

I Want to Swim

ABOUT THIS POEM

There isn't a person alive who doesn't aspire to achieve some goal that seems out of reach. Children are no exception, and they often keep their deepest wishes to themselves. Wish poems offer a perfect opportunity for exploration of their goals. Read "I Want to Swim" to students, and then ask them to share some of their wishes and dreams. You might create a list on the board as they volunteer how they've always wanted to ski, dance, or become a famous singer or sports star. If children have trouble finding an idea, ask them to think about the past and recall how they felt when they wanted to ride a two-wheeler or tie their shoes and couldn't!

SIMPLE WRITING STEPS

1 Ask students to choose their most interesting goal. Write the following poem model on the board:

I want to _____.
      (climb, sing, draw, whistle, and so on)

Really _____.

Not just _____

but _____.

Invite each child to fill in his or her goal. Encourage children to look back at the poem model for ideas.

2 To keep the poem moving, ask children to visualize themselves achieving the goal. Ask them: "What is your body doing? What next? What next?" Answering these questions will enable children to write the second stanza. For example:

    I want to play the flute,
    Really play the flute.
    I want to pucker up my lips and
    make the sweetest sound.

3 Encourage children to use the senses and imagine what they would see, hear, taste, or smell as they achieve their goal. The easiest way to do this is to write phrases on the board for kids to fill in, such as:

I'd see _____

I'd taste _____

I'd hear _____

I'd smell _____

4 Ask kids to imagine that they have accomplished their dream (they scored the winning goal in the World Cup finals, landed on the moon, and so on). How do they feel? What thoughts are going through their minds? They can start by filling in a simple phrase:

I feel_____

5 The ending belongs to the writer. It might simply be a restatement of the opening:

I want to _____.

Knoxville, Tennessee

I always like summer
best
you can eat fresh corn
from daddy's garden
and okra
and greens
and cabbage
and lots of
barbecue
and buttermilk
and homemade ice-cream
at the church picnic
and listen to
gospel music
outside
at the church
homecoming
and go to the mountains with
your grandmother
and go barefooted
and be warm
all the time
not only when you go to bed
and sleep

—Nikki Giovanni

Knoxville, Tennessee

ABOUT THIS POEM

How do poets create or re-create experiences for their listeners? Before reading "Knoxville, Tennessee" to your class, ask them to listen for the ways Nikki Giovanni brings her favorite season to life for the reader to experience. Write the words *eat*, *listen*, *go to*, and *be* on the board. Read the poem, and then ask children what they remember for each of these words. What did the poet eat? What did she listen to? Where did she go? Encourage students to talk about their favorite seasons. What do they like to eat, listen to, and do during their favorite time of year?

SIMPLE WRITING STEPS

1 First, ask students to choose their favorite season. Have them write a first line to introduce the season, such as:

> I love wintertime
>
> or
>
> Spring makes me the happiest

2 Next, have them brainstorm a list of at least five of their favorite foods to eat during their favorite season. (They can also include things to drink.) They can add some or all of these to the poem with a simple line such as:

> In the winter, I like to eat . . .

3 Ask them to think of at least five sounds they hear during their favorite season. Where do they hear these sounds? They can choose some of these to add to the poem. Then have them do the same with smells.

> I hear _____
>
> I smell _____

4 Invite students to choose some places they love to go during this time of year. They can also include who goes with them to these places:

> I love to visit _____ with
>
> _____

5 The last line is the clincher. Explain that until this point, their poem has been about the things they do during their favorite season. Encourage children to end the poem with a simple description of how they feel during this time of year. It's a good idea to have them reread their poems before they write the ending.

> I feel or I am _____
>
> (safe, sleepy, content, cozy, free, and so on)

Lapful of Lunes

lunes of description:

Round dustballs roll
under my brother's bed like
fuzzy gray spiders.

Snowflakes fall softly
on my mom's black car
like winter stars.

lunes of address:

Shine on me
all day old lady sun
because I'm cold.

Silver moon man—
sparkle through my window tonight.
Then I'll dream.

Tree, why do
they call you weeping willow?
Are you sad?

lunes of humor and situation:

Help! The stick
I just picked up is
starting to move.

Help! Soccerball is
soaring like a cannonball towards
the wrong goal.

—Maggie Flynn

Lapful of Lunes

The lune first appeared in the 1960s. It was the invention of poet Robert Kelly, who wanted to create a more Western form of haiku that used only 13 syllables instead of the traditional 17. The lune eventually evolved into its current and simpler form, which counts words instead of syllables. There are three words in the first line, five in the second, and three in the third. This makes the lune a perfect form for young writers because it's easier to count words than syllables. Another lure of the lune for children is that the subject matter is completely open!

SIMPLE WRITING STEPS

1 On the board, write one of the lunes and the pattern 3-5-3 beside it. Explain to students what a lune is. Read some lunes aloud, and then have kids count the words in each line.

2 Ask students to choose any subject for their own lune of description. Then ask them what this thing or person does. This forms the first line. Then ask them to answer the question *Where?* This forms the second line. Finally, children can write the last line by answering the question *How?* (Notice that the second and third lines are very simple prepositional phrases.)

Snowflakes fall softly	(thing/what it does)
on my mom's black car	(Where?)
like winter stars	(How? like…)

3 Read the lunes of address aloud. Then have children use the following model for writing their own lunes of address. Ask students to choose an object they'd like to talk to: A football? A star? The American flag? In their lune, they can ask the object a question or give it a command.

Silver moon man	(thing)
sparkle through my window tonight.	(command)
Then I'll dream.	(then I'll…)
Tree, why do	(thing)
they call you weeping willow?	(question)
Are you sad?	(question)

4 Funny situation lunes bring out the "loony lune" in all of us. Invite children to use the following model to write their own humorous lune.

Help! _____ _____	(thing)
_____ _____ _____ _____	(situation)
_____ _____ _____	(funny twist)

Fun 15-Minute Poetry-Writing Activities   Scholastic Professional Books

Rock and Rain

I used to be a boulder
but the rain came down.
I was big and round
but the rain came down.
I was hard and tough
but the rain came down.
At first I didn't notice any change
but the rain came down.
Centuries came and went
but the rain came down.
I became just a rock
but the rain came down.
That's enough, leave me alone I cried,
but the rain came down.
Even though it was soft and weak
the rain came down
and wore me into the ground,
and still the rain came down.

—Frank Asch

Rock and Rain

ABOUT THIS POEM

Frank Asch uses the repeated line "but the rain came down" as the foundation for this modern chant. The voice of this poem is a boulder that's been slowly weathered down to a rock. The repeated words (or refrain) reinforce the idea of repetitive rainfall. Invite kids to pinpoint their own subject: Dinosaurs? An ice cream cone? A caterpillar? A tornado? Brainstorm a few facts and adjectives about the subject to get the creative juices flowing, and then have kids get ready to speak for—and as—whatever object or creature they have chosen!

SIMPLE WRITING STEPS

1 Help children choose a subject for their poems by generating a list of topics together. Then have them introduce their subject in the first line.

> I was a _____.

(Some topics might tie in nicely with a science or social studies lesson. For example, "I was a famous leader" or "I was a caterpillar.")

2 Next, ask children to create their refrain: 'til the _____. Remind students that since this line will be repeated often, it should sound interesting and have a good rhythm. For example:

> I was an ice cream cone
> 'til the sun came out.

3 The rest is easy. Ask children to keep answering the question *What happened next?* after each line. Tell them to forget about the refrain for a moment and just write the factual lines. For example, *I was cold and sweet; I was chocolate and vanilla.*

4 After each child has written three to six facts (or more if desired), it's time to assemble their poems by inserting their refrain lines after each fact line.

> I was cold and sweet
> 'til the sun came out.
> I was chocolate and vanilla
> 'til the sun came out.

5 The ending is easy—just repeat the refrain!

Subway

Here come tiger down the track

ROAR-O

Big white eye and a mile-long back

ROAR-O

Through the darkest cave he run

ROAR-O

Never see the sky or sun

ROAR-O

—Lillian Morrison

Fun 15-Minute Poetry-Writing Activities Scholastic Professional Books

Subway

ABOUT THIS POEM

The exploration of chants and refrains would not be complete without a city poem. If children have never experienced a subway, they can experience it through their imaginations with the poem "Subway." Before you read the poem, ask children to imagine a one-eyed tiger hunting at night in the jungle. Tell them the tiger is running right toward them with its big eye glowing. Then ask them to picture this tiger changing into a subway train with one giant glowing light at the front. Ask kids to hear its loud roar as the train speeds through a dark tunnel. Then read the poem.

SIMPLE WRITING STEPS

1 Assist children in choosing an urban subject for their chant poems: A police car? A taxi? A crowded bridge? Buses? Crowds? A parade? A jackhammer? If students have only experienced a rural environment, ask them to picture machinery that they might be familiar with, such as a cement mixer or a tractor.

2 Once everyone has chosen a subject, invite children to picture it and then imagine it changing into something else—an animal or something surprising, strange, wild, or even funny.

3 Now children are ready for a first line. Here are some suggested openings in case they are stuck:

I see_____

I hear _____

Here comes _____

4 Next, ask children to make up a word or words to imitate the sound that their subject makes (for example, *clickety-clack* or *Hoooo-Y*). These words will become their chant, which they can repeat after every line.

5 Poems can be any length, alternating brief descriptive lines with chants. Children can end their poems with the chant, or they can choose another method. They might come up with an extra-fun sound for the very last line!

6 And the best part? Reading the poems aloud, of course!

Moon Poem

Moon rise
Moon light
Moon gleam
Moon bright

Moon trees
Moon pond
Moon silver
Moon swan

Moon hoot
Moon howl
Moon rustle
Moon growl

Moon snake
Moon breeze
Moon slither
Moon leaves

Moon house
Moon lawn
Moon freckles
Moon fawn

Moon window
Moon beam
Moon child
Moon dream

Moon eyes
Moon yawn
sun RISE
Moon

g
o
n
e

—Jacqueline Sweeney

Fun 15-Minute Poetry-Writing Activities Scholastic Professional Books

Moon Poem

ABOUT THIS POEM

"Moon Poem" is a list poem with a twist—its shape imitates its subject, a slant of moonlight! The repetition of the word *moon* throughout the poem also sets up an image pattern. The stanzas of four lines (or quatrains) allow for this seemingly fixed image, the moon, to move as it shines on whatever the author wishes. The fun of writing a poem like this is in compiling the list of things for the moon to shine upon.

SIMPLE WRITING STEPS

1 After reading the poem to your class, ask children to choose a subject that can physically interact with lots of things. You might compile a list of possible subjects to inspire students, such as the moon, sun, wind, snow, rain, fog, and so on.

2 Next, ask children to make a list of 10–20 objects or creatures their subject can shine or fall upon (or otherwise interact with). Ask them to close their eyes and pretend they're looking through a picture window. What do they see? Trees? Fields? A quiet town? An ocean? Animals? Habitats? These are some of the items they can add to their lists.

3 Give children a copy of "Moon Poem" to use as a model, and invite them to begin writing. Here are two sample beginnings for a poem about the sun. (Note: Verbs are optional, and poems do not have to rhyme!)

(Nonrhyming)		(Rhyming)
Sun morning		Sun orange
Sun orange	or	Sun rise
Sun shades		Sun open
Sun day		Sun eyes

4 Encourage kids to choose groups of four words that work together. Look back at "Moon Poem" to see how the four related words help create a scene. For example, the following stanza allows the reader to visualize an ocean scene:

Sun ocean
Sun roar
Sun crab
Sun shore

5 Allow children to write as many stanzas as they wish. Option: Once poems have been completed, you might suggest that children write them in a shape that reflects the subject in some way (an arc for a rainbow poem, an amorphous arrangement for fog, and so on).

January's a polar bear;
   February's a mole,
Fast asleep and dreaming
   Down a winter-dark hole.

March, the backyard robin,
   Struts up to April's worm,
Staring at a feast of spring,
   Daring him to squirm.

May's a monarch butterfly;
   June's a thousand bees,
Violining symphonies
   Under the linden trees.

July's one mad mosquito;
   Late August is a hawk,
Circling over summer and
   The summer-gone talk.

September is a school of fish;
   October's great horned owl
Eyes kindergarten goblins
   With a curious scowl.

November's the tom turkey
   We couldn't wait to roast,
But the deer that is December
   Is what I remember most.

—J. Patrick Lewis

Fun 15-Minute Poetry-Writing Activities   Scholastic Professional Books

January's a Polar Bear

Fun 15-Minute Poetry-Writing Activities   Scholastic Professional Books

ABOUT THIS POEM

This poem uses images to create word pictures for every month of the year, and it's a perfect vehicle for introducing metaphor to students. You might explain metaphors as a simple equation: January = a polar bear, February = a mole fast asleep, and so on. Point out that one side of the equation is a month of a year. The other side of the equation is a "word picture" composed of the sights, smells, tastes, and experiences that come from observation and memory. Your students can write their own sensational seasonal poems by first brainstorming a series of equations. When they replace the equal sign with the word *is*, they will have constructed a metaphor.

SIMPLE WRITING STEPS

1 Before reading the poem to children, explain that the author has created a word picture for every month of the year. Pause after reading each one and ask students to describe some different pictures that come from their own experiences of that particular month.

2 Next, ask children to use each month of the year in a simple equation. You might break your class into small groups and assign each three or four months.

    January = _____

    February = _____

    March = _____, and so on.

For a shorter poem, have children work with seasons instead of months.

    Summer = _____

    Autumn = _____

3 Ask children to fill in each equation with a detailed mind picture. Encourage them to take their time and use their senses to evoke tastes, smells, sounds, and so on.

4 Have children replace each equal sign with *is*. Encourage them to write one stanza for each month or season.

    January is _____

    February is _____

    _____ , and so on.

5 Children can add an interesting title (perhaps taken from a line in the poem) and share their poems aloud. Option: As a class, write a collaborative poem by brainstorming metaphors for the entire year. Copy the poem onto chart paper, have children add illustrations, and hang it in the hall for everyone to enjoy!

Good-by My Winter Suit

Good-by my winter suit,
good-by my hat and boot,
good-by my ear-protecting muffs
and storms that hail and hoot.

Farewell to snow and sleet,
farewell to Cream of Wheat,
farewell to ice-removing salt
and slush around my feet.

Right on! to daffodils,
right on! to whippoorwills,
right on! to chirp-producing eggs
and baby birds and quills.

The day is on the wing,
the kite is on the string,
the sun is where the sun should be—
it's spring all right! It's spring!

—N. M. Bodecker

Fun 15-Minute Poetry-Writing Activities Scholastic Professional Books

Good-by My Winter Suit

ABOUT THIS POEM

If you're studying seasons, or even just enjoying them, here is the poem for you! It's a fun way to say good-bye to one season while joyfully embracing the season ahead. And while you're at it, why not have a little multicultural language fun? Here's how:

SIMPLE WRITING STEPS

1. On chart paper, draw two columns. Label one "Hello" and the other "Good-bye." Beneath each heading, list ways to say hello and good-bye in different languages: *Hola—Adios, Bonjour—Adieu, Konnichiwa—Sayonara,* and so on. You might also add a few interesting English expressions: *Right on—Farewell, Hey there—'til next time,* and so on. Ask children for suggestions as you make the list.

2. Choose two seasons: One to say good-bye to and one to say hello to. Invite each child to brainstorm a list of at least ten season-specific characteristics for each. Direct children to think about categories such as weather, clothing, food, holidays, special events, pastimes, and so on. As always, encourage them to use their senses!

3. Write a simple structure on the chalkboard for children to use as a guide. They can decide which word or phrase for *good-bye* they wish to use. Children can then simply fill in the blanks with choices from their lists. (Their poems do not have to rhyme.)

   _____ to _____
   (Adios, farewell, and so on)
   _____ to _____
   (Sayonara, adieu)

   Repeat as often as desired. The poet can vary the good-bye words as he or she sees fit.

4. Now kids can greet the incoming season by filling in the blanks:

   _____ to _____
   (Right on, hola)
   _____ to _____ and so on.
   (Konnichiwa)

5. The ending should salute the incoming season. It might be one line or four, zany or serious—it's up to the writer! Encourage children to decide for themselves.

ACKNOWLEDGMENTS

Every effort has been made to trace copyright and we gratefully acknowledge the following permissions:

"Words" from A DIFFERENT WORLD: RHYMES TO READ by Jill Eggleton and Elizabeth Fuller. Published 1966 by The Wright Group, 19201 120th Avenue NE, Bothell, Washington 98011. (425) 486-8011. Reprinted by permission of the publisher.

"Our Washing Machine" from THE APPLE VENDOR'S FAIR by Patricia Hubbell. Copyright © 1963, 1991 by Patricia Hubbell. Used by permission of Marian Reiner for the author.

"Rain Drops" from THE RIDE HOME by Sallie Burrow Wood. Copyright © 1982 by Waterford Press.

"Sweets" from ALL THE SMALL POEMS AND FOURTEEN MORE by Valerie Worth. Copyright © 1987, 1994 by Valerie Worth. Reprinted by permission of Farrar, Straus and Giroux, LLC.

"Choose a Color" by Jacqueline Sweeney. Copyright © 1993 by Jacqueline Sweeney. Reprinted by permission of Marian Reiner for the author.

"Comida/Food" by Victor M. Valle from FIESTA IN AZTLAN. Reprinted by permission of Capra Press.

"The Blues" from COLLECTED POEMS by Langston Hughes. Copyright © 1994 by the Estate of Langston Hughes. Reprinted by permission of Alfred A. Knopf, a Division of Random House Inc.

"Street Song" from THE WAY THINGS ARE AND OTHER POEMS by Myra Cohn Livingston. Copyright © 1974 by Myra Cohn Livingston. Used by permission of Marian Reiner.

"Yellow Weed" from LITTLE RACCOON AND POEMS FROM THE WOODS by Lilian Moore. Copyright © 1975 by Lilian Moore. Used by permission of Marian Reiner for the author.

"Letter to Bee" from THE POEMS OF EMILY DICKINSON edited by Ralph W. Franklin, Cambridge, Mass.: The Belknap Press of Harvard University Press. Copyright © 1998 by the President and Fellows of Harvard College. Copyright © 1951, 1955, 1979 by the President and Fellows of Harvard College. Reprinted by permission of the publishers and the Trustees of Amherst College.

"The Inchworm" from INSECTLOPEDIA by Douglas Florian. Copyright © 1998 by Douglas Florian. Reprinted with permission of Harcourt, Inc.

"Topsy-Turvy Land" by H. E. Wilkinson appeared in BOOK OF 1000 POEMS, HarperCollins Publishers, London.

"Sky" from COME ON INTO MY TROPICAL GARDEN by Grace Nichols (A & C Black, 1988). Copyright Grace Nichols 1988. Reprinted with permission of Curtis Brown Ltd, London on behalf of Grace Nichols.

"whispers" by Monica Kulling. Copyright © 2000 by Monica Kulling. Used by permission of Marian Reiner for the author.

"I Want You to Meet" from TAKE SKY by David McCord. Copyright © 1961, 1962 by David McCord. By permission of Little, Brown and Company (Inc.).

"Rules" from ALEXANDER SOAMES: HIS POEMS by Karla Kuskin. Copyright © 1962, 1980 by Karla Kuskin. Reprinted by permission of Scott Treimel New York.

"Mixed-Up Me" by Wyoming. Reprinted by permission of the author.

"I Want to Swim" by Jacqueline Sweeney. Copyright © 1996 by Jacqueline Sweeney. First published in Spider. Reprinted by permission of Marian Reiner for the author.

"Knoxville, Tennessee" from BLACK FEELING, BLACK TALK, BLACK JUDGMENT by Nikki Giovanni. Copyright © 1968, 1970 by Nikki Giovanni. Reprinted by permission of HarperCollins Publishers, Inc. (William Morrow)

"Lapful of Lunes" by Maggie Flynn. Copyright © 2000 by Maggie Flynn. Used by permission of Marian Reiner for the author.

"Rock and Rain" from COUNTRY PIE by Frank Asch. Copyright © 1979 by Frank Asch. Used by permission of HarperCollins Publishers.

"Subway" by Lillian Morrison. Copyright © 1979 by Lillian Morrison. Used by permission of Marian Reiner for the author.

"Moon Poem" by Jacqueline Sweeney. Copyright © 2000 by Jacqueline Sweeney. Reprinted by permission of Marian Reiner for the author.

Excerpt from untitled poem which begins "January's a polar bear; February's a mole…" from JULY IS A MAD MOSQUITO by J. Patrick Lewis. Copyright ©1994 by J. Patrick Lewis. Reprinted with the permission of Atheneum Books for Young Readers, an imprint of Simon & Schuster Children's Publishing Division.

"Good-by My Winter Suit" from HURRY, HURRY, MARY DEAR! AND OTHER NONSENSE POEMS by N. M. Bodecker. Copyright © 1976 by N. M. Bodecker. Reprinted with permission of Margaret K. McElderry Books, an imprint of Simon & Schuster Children's Publishing Division.

Fun 15-Minute Poetry-Writing Activities   Scholastic Professional Books